Published by Creative Education
123 South Broad Street, Mankato, Minnesota 56001
Creative Education is an imprint of The Creative Company

Art direction by Rita Marshall
Production design by The Design Lab

Smart Apple 17-03/24.22- 16.95

Library of Congress Cataloging-in-Publication Data

Hidalgo, Maria.
Water / by Maria Hidalgo.
p. cm. — (Let's investigate)
Summary: Presents information on the properties of water, the
hydrologic cycle, oceans, rain and snow, and the importance of
water to living things.
ISBN 1-58341-229-8
1. Water—Juvenile literature. [1. Water.] I. Title. II. Series.
GB662.3 .H54   2002
551.46—dc21   2001047891

First edition

2   4   6   8   9   7   5   3   1

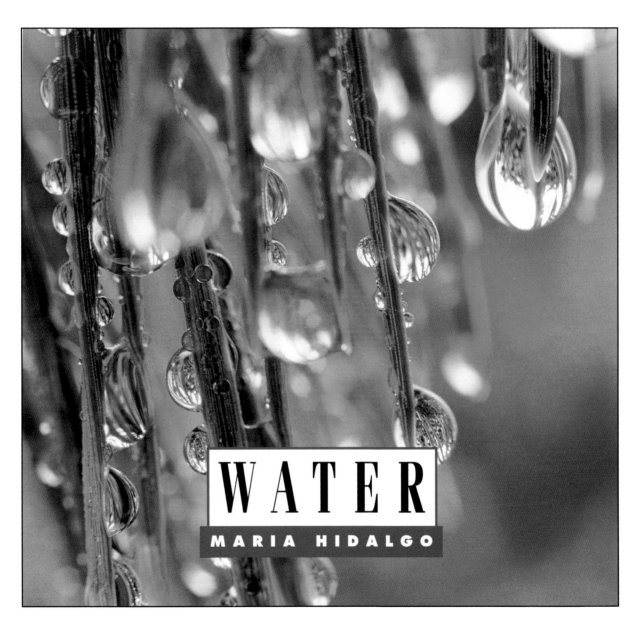

WATER

MARIA HIDALGO

Creative ◆ Education

WATER
WALKERS

Fishing spiders can actually walk on water. They are so light that the links between water mole-cules can support them. Plus, a waxy substance keeps their feet dry!

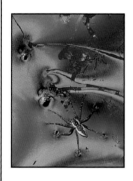

Above, a fishing spider Right, antelope at a watering hole

We live in a world of water. Covering nearly three-quarters of the earth, water is the most **abundant** substance on our planet's surface. About 326 million cubic miles (1.4 billion cu km) of water exist in our oceans, lakes, streams, glaciers, and **ground-water**. And since it makes up more than 70 percent of the weight of living organisms, water is **indispensable** to survival on Earth.

WATER
WEIGHT

When water freezes, the solid ice weighs as much as the liquid did. When the ice melts, the weight remains unchanged. This is called "conservation of mass."

WATER
COVERAGE

Glaciers are enormous masses of ice that stay frozen all year round and cover about 11 percent of the world's land area.

Icebergs are floating ice chunks that have broken away from glaciers

FORMS OF WATER

Water is a combination of two elements, hydrogen and oxygen, and is often represented by the scientific symbol H_2O. It exists in three forms, or states: liquid, solid, or gas. Most of Earth's water exists as a liquid, largely as fresh groundwater or salty ocean water. Water in its solid state is known as ice. Ice is found in glaciers and the great polar ice sheets, such as Antarctica. These huge ice formations store more than 90 percent of Earth's freshwater. As a gas, such as steam, water molecules scatter throughout the air and can be either hot or cold.

Humidity measures how much water vapor is in the air. Relative humidity compares the amount of moisture in the air with the most humidity that can exist at that temperature.

Atoms and molecules, such as the ones that make up water, are always in motion. When water is a solid, the atoms are close together and barely vibrate. When water is a liquid, the molecules have more energy and can slide past each other. Some molecules build up enough energy through heat or pressure to escape in gas form.

Clouds of condensed water vapor called fog

WATER
CONCERN

Global warming is affecting Earth's water supply, continually melting inland glaciers as well as the ice sheets of Antarctica and Greenland.

WATER
GIANTS

Icebergs form when chunks of glaciers break off into the sea. These massive, floating bodies of freshwater ice hide up to 85 percent of their size below the ocean's surface.

Melting icebergs changing from solid forms to liquid

Water can move from one state to another; all it needs is the right environment. There are two **crucial** points where water changes form: the boiling point and the melting point.

The boiling point—the condition at which liquid water becomes a gas—is not simply the temperature at which water boils (212 °F (100 °C)). The boiling point can also be caused by pressure. Pressure can compress liquid water molecules enough to give them the energy to vaporize, releasing them into the air and turning them into gas molecules. This is also known as the condensing point because it is the exact level of pressure at which vapor (such as steam or **condensation**) turns back into liquid again.

WATER
CONDENSATION

Drops of water that appear on the outside of a cold can or glass are the result of invisible water vapor in the air condensing (turning into a liquid) on the colder surface.

WATER
WHISTLE

Water vapor expands when it is warm. That's why a hot teakettle's whistle blows: the steam inside the kettle cannot be contained and must escape.

A geyser shoots hot water and steam from the ground into the air

WATER

CONDUCTOR

Sound waves travel better underwater than they do through air, moving at speeds more than three times as fast.

WATER

TEMPERATURE

Pure water freezes at 32 °F (0 °C) and boils at 212 °F (100 °C). When salt is added, the freezing point falls and the boiling point rises.

Icicles form when dripping water freezes

The melting point marks the line between solid and liquid. Ice turns to water when the temperature is above 32 °F (0 °C). At exactly 32 °F (0 °C), both water and ice can exist. When water is in its solid state, it shares many properties with other solids, such as the way it holds a permanent three-dimensional shape. Once water turns into a liquid or gas, however, it is capable of moving and changing form, depending on its surroundings.

WATER

MOVEMENT

As the moon orbits Earth and Earth orbits the sun, gravitational forces from the heavenly bodies pull Earth's water toward the sky, causing high and low tides.

WATER

WAVES

Tsunamis, also known as tidal waves or seismic sea waves, are huge waves caused by underwater earthquakes and volcanic eruptions.

Anytime water changes states, conservation of energy occurs. This means that the same amount of energy always exists, no matter what form the water takes. For example, when water boils into steam, all of the heat energy used to make the water boil becomes energy in the gas.

Wind blowing across the ocean surface creates waves

WATER

FACT

A damp surface dries quicker when a fan blows on it because the water molecules absorb energy from the moving air and use it to "jump" off the surface.

12

Earth's water cycle begins with the ocean

THE WATER CYCLE

The three forms of water appear in nature as the water cycle, also called the hydrologic cycle. Water vapor evaporates from oceans, groundwater, and freshwater sources, such as lakes and rivers. Air currents carry the water vapor high into the air, where it cools and condenses into clouds. The clouds then cool enough to create precipitation, which is water in any form returning to Earth, such as rain, snow, hail, or mist.

Once the water is on land again, it collects in lakes, rivers, soil, and rocks underground. It drains to the ocean and begins the cycle again. About 26,390 cubic miles (110,000 cu km) of rain fall on land each year after spending about a week and a half in the air. As the water travels from Earth to the sky and back again, it dissolves minerals, gases, organic substances, and even bacteria, and carries them along for the ride.

WATER VAPOR

Steam is visible water vapor. There is invisible water vapor in steam too, but it is mixed with tiny droplets of water that make the steam look white.

13

WATER
POLLUTION

Frog and amphibian species around the world are disappearing. These animals breathe through their skin, and pollution in water has a particularly harmful effect on their health.

14

An unpolluted fresh-water river in the Pacific Northwest

reshwater can be depleted. In addition, human pollution can add undesirable ingredients to freshwater, such as chemicals from fertilizers, **herbicides**, and **pesticides**. Pollution can make water sources unusable, even with the best cleaning treatments available. This limits the amount of drinking water available and adds harmful elements to the water cycle.

WATER
NEIGHBORS

Freshwater and salt water can exist at the same time in the same area; for instance, during warm seasons, glaciers melt into the ocean and float freshwater on the surface.

All animal life native to the sea has evolved to survive in the ocean's salty surroundings. These animals are either able to drink seawater and excrete the salt or able to get their water by eating non-salty foods. Ocean water has been mixing and churning for so long that its salt content is the same anywhere in the world, so ocean-dwelling fish, amphibians, and mammals do not need to adapt to new salt levels as they travel great distances in search of food or mates.

Dolphins thrive in the ocean's salty water

WATER
POLLUTION

Acid rain is precipitation that has been polluted by sulfur dioxide and nitrogen oxides from burning fuels. The effects of acid rain include shrinking fish populations and forest ecosystem damage.

Fishermen casting their lines into the fog-covered sea

WATER IN OCEANS

Early in its formation, Earth did not have water on its surface. The first appearance of water probably came from three sources: the rocks that make up the bulk of the planet, **meteorites** that crashed into Earth, and **comets** that also collided with Earth's surface. As Earth formed, great heat was generated. This heat caused different elements and compounds to form, and created the **hydrosphere** and the **atmosphere** at the same time. Eventually, the

earth's surface cooled, and water could exist as a liquid as well as a gas.

Water in the ocean has much to do with weather around the world. When the sun heats ocean water, water vapor is added to the air through **evaporation**. This warm water vapor strengthens updrafts by causing heated air to rise. Cooler air flows in below and creates gentle breezes and powerful winds.

Pacific salmon are born in freshwater streams. As the fish grow, they develop the ability to survive in salty ocean water as well.

Above, pink salmon swimming upstream to spawn

W A T E R
SCULPTORS

Waves are caused by winds, tides, and currents, and play an important part in reshaping Earth, eroding (breaking down) and rebuilding coastlines.

Above, beach sand sculpted by waves
Right, a hurricane as seen from space
Far right, violent waves

Heat from the ocean also transfers to the air during evaporation. When the water on the surface of the ocean cools, it becomes heavier than the warmer water around it and flows down, creating a circular water current. Wind also causes ocean currents, pushing the water along the surface and, in turn, disrupting water farther below.

When enough hot air rises quickly enough, it creates low-pressure systems that can cause severe storms called hurricanes or typhoons. Hurricanes and typhoons can be as large as 500 miles (800 km) wide, with winds as high as 100 miles (160 km) per hour.

WATER
COLOR

Red tides, crimson-colored areas of water in the ocean, are caused by excessive amounts of blooming single-celled algae.

WATER
STORMS

Hurricanes usually hit coastlines along the Atlantic Ocean because they tend to travel west-northwest. The Gulf Stream also adds a lot of thermal energy to the creation of hurricanes.

Water evaporates easily from calm, warm waters and forms clouds

When sea surface temperatures are higher than normal along the equator in the Pacific Ocean, a weather condition known as El Niño occurs. This usually happens every three to seven years. Slowed-down trade winds result in a calmer water surface. Calmer water means the surface remains warmer (since below-surface cool water doesn't get mixed in) and adds extra water vapor to the air. This sends tropical storms over a larger area than usual, even causing storms on the other side of the world.

WATER
LEVEL

If only 10 percent of all the frozen glacier and ice shelf water on Earth melted into the ocean, sea level would rise by 20 feet (6.1 m).

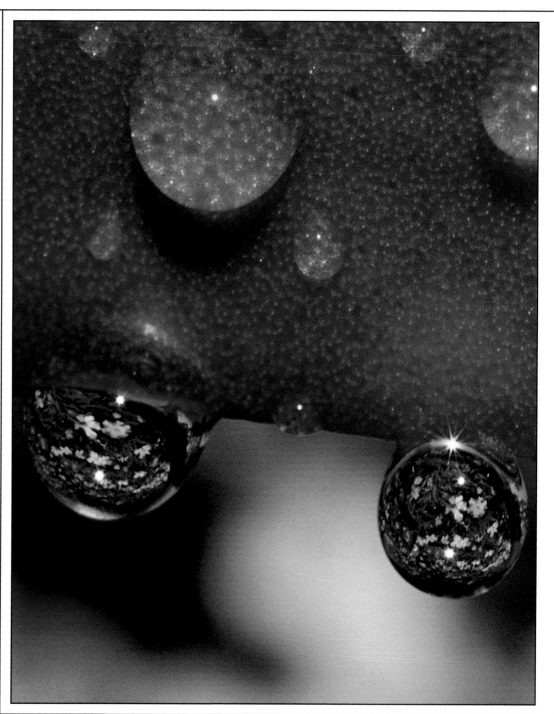

Above, icebergs
Right, a colorful garden reflected off raindrops

When iron is exposed to the oxygen in water, a layer of iron oxide and hydroxide, called rust, develops on its surface.

23

RAIN AND SNOW

Billions upon billions of **microscopic** water droplets and ice bits create the clouds that float overhead. Each cloud, even though it carries tons of water, stays in the air because the water particles are so tiny. The water does not fall until the droplets condense into a single raindrop heavy enough for gravity to affect it. One raindrop usually contains one million droplets!

Precipitation comes in many forms. The most common is rain, which can offer crop-saving moisture to farms one day and cause devastating flooding the next day. The wettest known point on Earth is Mount Waialeale in Hawaii. An average of 460 inches (1,170 cm) of rain falls each year.

Above, rusty iron gears Left, water returning to Earth as rain

WATER

FACT

Water will cause stainless steel to rust, but the metal contains elements that keep the rust layer extremely thin, so to the naked eye, the rust never appears at all.

Water in the air helps create rainbows

During or after a rainstorm, rainbows can often be seen in the sky directly opposite from the sun. Light from the sun shines through each individual raindrop, which **refracts** each color in the light in a slightly different direction. The separated light colors can be seen by the human eye and always line up in the same order: red, orange, yellow, green, blue, indigo, and violet.

I f air temperatures are cold enough, snowflakes rather than raindrops drift to Earth. Always hexagonal (six-sided) and **symmetrical**, snowflakes are caused by water molecules aligning to fit perfectly together, with changes in temperature and humidity causing pattern differences in the snowflakes as they drift downward. Since no two journeys from cloud to Earth are the same, every snowflake is different.

When water freezes, it expands, becomes less dense, and therefore floats on top of liquid water. Ice floes and icebergs are good examples of this property.

25

Above, a seal resting on an ice floe
Left, heavy, wet snow and ice

WATER
CHILL

When coming out of a shower or swimming pool, people often feel chilly. That's because energy in the form of heat escapes as the water evaporates from their skin.

WATER AND LIFE

The human body is made up of 60 to 75 percent water. And while most adults could live without food for a while, the longest they could survive without water is less than five days. Every cell and organ process in humans, animals, and plants depends on water to function correctly.

Plants need water to grow and bloom

27

Water transports nutrients to every part of an organism, keeps waste moving through the intestinal tract, and creates a protective covering around important organs. In humans, water cushions the brain, eyes, and spinal cord. Water regulates body temperature as well, with up to a pint of perspiration cooling a human's body on an average day—even more during hot days and exercise. The same is true of animals, although their perspiration is often hidden under layers of fur.

An elephant drinking water to stay cool

WATER
FITNESS

Swimming is excellent exercise, not just because it uses every muscle group in the body, but also because water produces 1,000 times more drag resistance than air, forcing muscles to work harder.

WATER
DISINFECTANT

Chlorine, one of the earth's basic elements, is often used to disinfect drinking and swimming water, as it kills microorganisms that can cause disease.

A pitcher of clean drinking water

An adult needs at least six eight-ounce (240 ml) glasses of water each day. This replaces the fluid lost each day as sweat, exhaled air, urine, and bowel movements. While other beverages such as juice or milk do deliver water to a body, the best source of water is water itself. Drinking water is piped into homes from freshwater sources that have been treated to remove harmful microorganisms and chemicals. Fine screens remove particles; chlorine, ozone, and ultraviolet radiation are used as disinfectants.

Bottlenose dolphins can sleep in water without drowning because the two sides of their brain take turns staying awake to watch for predators and to trigger breathing.

29

P lants also depend on water circulation to survive. Trees transport water to their uppermost branches in two ways. Fluid absorbed by roots creates pressure that pushes water to the top of the tree. In addition, as water evaporates from the canopy (the leaves forming the top cover of the tree), suction is created at a cellular level. Higher cells pull water from the layer below them; leaves pull from twigs, twigs from branches, and so on, all the way down to water at ground level.

*Above, a dolphin
Left, a forest of healthy plant life*

WATER

SALT

Ocean water everywhere around the world contains about 3.5 percent dissolved salt, whereas freshwater rivers contain only about 0.012 percent salt.

WATER

FACT

Since the Great Salt Lake in Utah has no place for water to drain, its water contains three to nine times more salt than ocean water does.

A family watching the sun set over Utah's Great Salt Lake

Water is the earth's lifeblood, a necessary resource for all living things, and must be treated with care. At each stage of the hydrologic cycle, water serves as a nutrient as well as an environment, supporting life in its many and varied forms. Only by keeping existing water supplies unpolluted (as well as protecting Earth's natural reserves) can we be sure that there will be enough clean water to drink, to grow food, and to take care of all future life on Earth.

Glossary

Something is **abundant** if there is plenty of it.

The **atmosphere** is the thick mass of air that surrounds Earth; it's held in place by gravity.

Comets are small celestial bodies that orbit the sun and occasionally collide with Earth's atmosphere.

Condensation is the process of changing from a gas to a liquid, such as when steam condenses on a bathroom mirror.

If something is very important or significant, it is **crucial**.

Evaporation is the process of changing from a liquid to a gas.

Groundwater is water that exists below Earth's surface, filling spaces between soil and rocks.

Herbicides are chemicals, natural or artificial, used to kill unwanted plants.

The **hydrosphere** is all of the earth's water, including water vapor, oceans, rivers, lakes, groundwater, glaciers, and ice shelves.

Something is **indispensable** if there is no substitute, or if it is absolutely essential to life.

Meteorites are particles of matter from space that reach the surface of Earth without being completely vaporized in Earth's atmosphere.

Microscopic objects or creatures are so small they can be seen only with the help of a microscope.

Pesticides are chemicals, natural or artificial, used to kill unwanted organisms, usually insects.

When a light wave **refracts**, it bends.

If a **symmetrical** object is split down the middle, both halves will be identical in size and shape.

Index

Photographs by Affordable Photo Stock (Francis & Donna Caldwell), Corbis (David Muench), Eyewire, Gregory Fischer, Dennis Frates, The Image Finders (Kenny Bahr, Jim Baron), KAC Productions (Larry Ditto, Greg W. Lasley), Paul T. McMahon, Tom Myers, Photo Researchers (Michael Lustbader), Tom Stack & Associates (Thomas Kitchin, Kitchin & Hurst, Gary Milburn, Doug Sokell, TSADO/NOAA/NCDC, Greg Vaughn, Dave Watts), Unicorn Stock Photos (Doug Adams, Robert E. Barber, Chris Boylan), Weatherstock (Warren Faidley)